C000193558

WEST YORKSHIRE BUSES IN TRANSITION

BEFORE AND AFTER WYPTE

KEITH W. PLATT

AMBERLEY

First published 2020

Amberley Publishing
The Hill, Stroud
Gloucestershire, GL5 4EP

www.amberley-books.com

Copyright © Keith W. Platt, 2020

The right of Keith W. Platt to be identified as
the Author of this work has been asserted in
accordance with the Copyrights, Designs and
Patents Act 1988.

ISBN 978 1 4456 9666 9 (print)
ISBN 978 1 4456 9667 6 (ebook)

All rights reserved. No part of this book may be
reprinted or reproduced or utilised in any form
or by any electronic, mechanical or other means,
now known or hereafter invented, including
photocopying and recording, or in any information
storage or retrieval system, without the permission
in writing from the Publishers.

British Library Cataloguing in Publication Data.
A catalogue record for this book is available from
the British Library.

Typesetting by Aura Technology and Software
Services, India. Printed in UK.

Introduction

The reorganisation of local government in England, from 1974, had been brought about by the Local Government Act of 1972. West Yorkshire became one of the newly created metropolitan councils and was responsible for running transport operations in its area. On 1 April 1974 the West Yorkshire Passenger Transport Executive was created by merging the municipal bus fleets of Bradford City Transport and Halifax Corporation with Calderdale Joint Omnibus Committee, Huddersfield Corporation and Leeds City Transport.

The new Transport Executive was divided into four districts: Bradford, Calderdale (previously Halifax and Todmorden), Kirklees (previously Huddersfield) and Leeds. A new livery of cream and light green slowly but surely began to replace the blue and cream of Bradford, the orange, green and cream of Halifax, the red and cream of Huddersfield, and the two shades of green of Leeds. With over 1,500 vehicles and more than 6,000 staff, along with the numerous garage and depot facilities, this was a huge operation.

By 1976 changes were being made to the livery. While retaining the colour scheme, much of the lining details were replaced and the district name under the Metro logo gave way to Metrobus.

The photographs in the book illustrate this process of absorption of the bus fleets of Bradford, Halifax, Huddersfield and Leeds from before 1974 up to the end of the decade.

All the photographs in this book are from my original collection with the exception of those belonging to the archive of Doncaster Omnibus & Light Railway Society. I would like to thank Eric Moy, Vice-Chair of DO&LRS, for making these images available and Jim Sambrooks, Chair of DO&LRS, for his help with information about various vehicle histories. I would also like to thank my brother, J. B. Platt, for all the proofreading he has undertaken and finally my wife, Andrea, for her help with solutions to numerous IT issues.

August 1964, Sunbeam F4 FWX 913 in Forster Square
FWX 913 was a 1948 Sunbeam F4, new to Mexborough & Swinton with a centre-entrance Brush B32C body. It was re-seated to B35C in 1956. It was bought by Bradford City Transport after the closure of the system and rebodied by East Lancs, in 1962, with an 8-foot-wide H37/29F body. Although purchased for preservation in 1973, it jack-knifed with its tow wagon while being towed to the Trolleybus Museum at Sandtoft. It was initially repaired using the front end of trolleybus 843. The body was eventually scrapped in 1979 and the chassis displayed at the museum. An individual had plans to re-body the chassis to its original Mexborough & Swinton condition, but the chassis was so corroded it too was eventually scrapped. In this image the Forster Square redevelopment was already underway, and the trolleybus route altered accordingly.

September 1964, AEC 661T CAK 674 on Broadway
CAK 674 was an AEC 661T, new to Bradford City Transport in May 1939 with an English Electric H30/26R body. It was fitted with an 8-foot-wide H35/28R body by East Lancs, re-entering service in June 1956. 674 was photographed here at the rear of the ABC Ritz, on Leeds Road, in its final year of service.

October 1964, Karrier W CBX 531 in Hall Ings
CBX 531 was a Karrier W delivered new to Llanelly & District Traction Company in 1945. Bradford City Transport acquired the chassis only from South Wales Transport, Swansea, in January 1953 and had it re-bodied by East Lancs with an 8-foot-wide H35/26R body. It entered service in February 1953 and was eventually sold for scrap in August 1971. It is seen on the Buttershaw service leaving the city centre in Hall Ings with St George's Hall behind the rear of the trolleybus.

October 1964, EKU 543 and EKU 750 at Thornbury Works
EKU 750 was a BUT 9611T with a Roe H31/25R body. It was delivered new to Bradford City Transport in December 1949, one of a batch of twelve similar vehicles. It became the first withdrawal from the group following a collision in 1963. It seems amazing given the bodywork damage that there was only one broken window. It awaits its fate in the yard at the back of Thornbury Works. EKU 543 was an AEC Regent III, which had been new to Bradford in 1948 along with eleven others. It had been withdrawn in 1961 and its H30/26R Northern Coach Builders body converted for use as a pole painter's wagon. It was finally withdrawn from these duties in March 1972.

October 1964, BUT 9611T NNU 237 at Thornbury Works
NNU 237 was a BUT 9611T with a Weymann H30/26R body. It had been delivered new to Nottinghamshire & Derbyshire Traction Company in May 1949. All thirty-two trolleybuses of this company's fleet were purchased by Bradford in 1953 and some entered service straight away, retaining their deep blue livery for a year or so. 773 had been withdrawn in 1963 but would stay at Thornbury Works, providing spare parts for the operating fleet, until it was finally scrapped in June 1967.

September 1965, BUT 9611T BDJ 86 at Holme Wood
BDJ 86 was a BUT 9611T with an East Lancs H35/28R body. It had been delivered new to St Helens Corporation Transport in January 1951 and bought by Bradford City Transport in 1958. It was one of eight similar vehicles from St Helens which, before entering service with Bradford, had their bodies renovated by Roe and then re-seated with increased capacity. 798 was photographed working an enthusiasts' special for the National Trolleybus Association and is seen on Bradford's last new trolleybus route to the Holme Wood estate, which was opened March 1960 as route 17. At the terminus the trolleybuses used a reverser, the only one in Bradford in use regularly.

March 1968, Karrier W DKY 707 at Bradford Moor
DKY 707 is seen at the Thornbury (Bradford Moor) terminus of route 7. It was a Karrier W delivered new to Bradford City Transport in July 1945 with a Roe H30/26R body. In the summer of 1960, it was rebodied with an eight-foot wide H37/29F East Lancs body and remained in service until 1971. It was scrapped two years later. The Daimler CRG6LX, FKY 272E, with a Metro-Cammell H43/31F body had been delivered new a year earlier and would pass into the fleet of West Yorkshire PTE as their 2272 in April 1974.

August 1968, BUT 9611T EKU 745, Little Horton Lane, Bradford
EKU 745 was a BUT 9611T with a Roe H31/25R body, one of twelve similar vehicles delivered new to Bradford City Transport in December 1949. It was the last of the batch to remain in service, being withdrawn in May 1971 and scrapped the following year. It is seen on Little Horton Lane, opposite Chester Street bus station, soon after returning to passenger-carrying after a four-year stint as a tuition vehicle, No. 060.

October 1968, AEC Regent III HLX 233, Ravenscliffe terminus
HLX 233 was Bradford Corporation Transport 419 and had been new to London Transport in September 1947 as RT416, an AEC Regent III with a Park Royal H30/26R body. It was one of twenty RTs purchased by Bradford Corporation in May 1958 in order to replace the remaining utility vehicles in the fleet. It was withdrawn a few weeks after this photograph, in 1968, and scrapped the following year. It is seen turning at the Ravenscliffe estate terminus.

October 1968, HLX 233 and YAK 128, Ravenscliffe terminus
HLX 233 was Bradford City Transport 419. It was one of twenty RTs purchased by Bradford Corporation in May 1958. They were little altered from their original condition other than a new livery and most, like 419, had their roof-box indicators removed. The bus in front, just departing the Ravenscliffe estate terminus, was YAK 128, a 1962 AEC Regent V with a Metro-Cammell H39/31F body, which would enter the fleet of West Yorkshire PTE in April 1974.

June 1969, LAK 328G, Leeds Central Bus Station
LAK328G was a Daimler Fleetline CRG6LX with an Alexander H43/31F body. It was one of a batch of twenty similar buses delivered new to Bradford City Transport at the end of 1968. They were all taken into the fleet of West Yorkshire Passenger Transport Executive in April 1974.

July 1969, Leyland PD2 EKY 558, Haworth
EKY 558 was one of four all-Leyland PD2s purchased by Bradford City Transport in July 1949. The seating capacity was increased from fifty-six to sixty seats in 1956. It was withdrawn from service in 1968 and set aside for preservation and is seen here in Haworth, West Yorkshire, with an enthusiasts' outing. (Photograph M. Fowler)

July 1970, BUT 9611T EKU 746, Bradford City Centre
EKU 746 was another BUT 9611T with a Roe H31/25R body, one of twelve similar vehicles delivered new to Bradford City Transport in December 1949. In December 1966 it became a tuition vehicle and was renumbered 063. It had the distinction of being used for the last trolleybus driving test in July 1971 and was subsequently privately preserved. It is now operational on the circuit of the Trolleybus Museum at Sandtoft.

June 1971, Sunbeam F4 JWW 377, heading for Greengates
JWW 377 was a 1950 Sunbeam F4 new to Mexborough & Swinton. It was one of a batch of chassis-only purchases by Bradford City Transport and one of the seven, rebodied by East Lancs in 1962, with an 8-foot-wide H37/29F body. It was to remain in service up to the end of trolleybus operations in Bradford in March 1972 and was then preserved. It now awaits restoration at the Trolleybus Museum at Sandtoft.

June 1971, BUT 9611T FKU 758, Laisterdyke
FKU 758 was a BUT 9611T with a Weymann H30/26R body, one of eight similar vehicles delivered new to Bradford City Transport in late 1950 and early 1951. In May 1952, 758 had been fitted with experimental flashing indicators, the first legal use of flashing indicators in Britain. This vehicle continued to operate until 31 July 1971, becoming the last rear-entrance trolleybus in service in the British Isles, after which it was secured for preservation. It is presently undergoing restoration at Keighley Bus Museum.

July 1971, BUT 9611T LHN 781, passing under Pasture Lane Bridge
LHN 781 was a 1949 BUT 9611T delivered new to Darlington Corporation. It was one of five trolleybuses which had been bought and operated by Doncaster Corporation Transport in 1952. By 1959 they had been sold again to Bradford City Transport and their East Lancs 7-foot 6-inch bodies scrapped. The chassis were renovated and modified to be rebodied with new 8-foot East Lancs H37/29F bodies. It is seen passing under Pasture Lane railway bridge en route to Clayton after leaving the Pasture Lane turning circle. Forty-eight years after this image was taken the subject on the billboard remains very topical. (Photograph L. Flint)

June 1971, BDJ 87, CBX 912 and DKY 717 inside Thornbury Depot
BDJ 87 was a 1951 ex-St Helens Corporation BUT 9611T with an East Lancs
H35/28R body. Along with seven similar vehicles, it was bought by Bradford City
Transport in 1958. After having had their bodies and seats renovated by Roe, they
entered service. CBX 912 was a 1945 ex-South Wales Transport Company Karrier W,
which had been acquired with nine others by Bradford in 1952 as a chassis only. They
received new East Lancs 8-foot-wide H35/28RD bodies. DKY 717 was a Karrier W
delivered new to Bradford City Transport in 1945. In the summer of 1960, it was
rebodied with an 8-foot-wide H37/29F East Lancs body. (Photograph M. Fowler)

June 1971, YKW 148, outside Bradford Thornbury Depot
YKW 148 was an AEC Regent V with a Metropolitan-Cammell H40/30F body. It was
one of sixty similar vehicles purchased by Bradford City Transport in 1963. All of
these buses were to pass to West Yorkshire PTE in April 1974; YKW 148 received its
new owner's livery soon afterwards. (Photograph M. Fowler)

September 1971, Withdrawn LeylandPD2/3 GKU 57 and AEC Regent III FKY 13, Thornbury
Bradford AEC Regent III FKY 13 with a Weymann H33/26R body had been new to Bradford
City Transport in 1949. It was withdrawn from service in 1969 and removed for scrap
days after the photograph had been taken. GKU 57 was a LeylandPD2/3 with a Leyland
H33/26R body of 1950 vintage. It was withdrawn in 1967 but was not removed for scrap
until May 1972.

September 1971, 6213 KW at the Clayton Trolleybus Terminus
6213 KW was one of thirty similar AEC Regent Vs with Metro-Cammell H40/30F bodies.
It was delivered new to Bradford Corporation Transport in March 1964. It waits in the terminus
loop of trolleybus route 37, to Clayton, at the top of The Avenue, next to Clayton Lane junction.
The trolleybus operations had ended on this part of the route on 31 May 1970. Now only the
poles and wires remain as a sad reminder of the efficient, low-polluting passenger transport
system. (Photograph L. Flint)

26 March 1972, FWX 914 at Four Lane Ends on the Last Day
FWX 914 was a 1948 Sunbeam F4. It had been new to Mexborough & Swinton and the chassis was bought by Bradford City Transport and rebodied by East Lancs, in 1962, with an 8-foot-wide H37/29F body. It was chosen to perform the last trolleybus duties on the final day and was suitably decorated for the occasion. Four Lane Ends had been the scene of a tragic accident involving a trolleybus in August 1970; the booms were pulled from the wires and crashed against a pole, the broken ends fell on and killed two young boys who had been sitting on a seat outside the Craven Heifer. (Photograph L. Flint)

June 1972, AEC Regent V MCW YAK 135, Bradford
YAK 135 was the last of ten AEC Regent Vs with Metropolitan-Cammell bodies which had been delivered to Bradford Corporation Transport in November 1962. All of these vehicles were transferred to the fleet of West Yorkshire PTE in April 1974 and had their fleet numbers prefixed with the number '2'.

June 1972, AEC Regent III HKW 86, Ings Hall
HKW 86 was an AEC Regent III 9613E with an East Lancashire H33/28R body. It was one of a batch of eighteen delivered new in 1952, all of which were re-seated in 1957 to 35/26. A severe shortage of buses in 1967 meant that ten of the batch, including HKW 86, were selected for overhaul rather than withdrawal. It was in its last week of service, in 1972, when photographed in Ings Hall. It was finally sold for scrap in February 1974. (Photograph B. Ridge)

June 1972, AEC Regent Vs 2172 KW and PKY 120 Await their Next Duty
2172 KW was an AEC Regent V with a H40/30F body, one out of several batches delivered to Bradford City Transport during 1963 which totalled sixty vehicles. PKY 120 was the last of fifteen AEC Regent Vs with H39/31F Metro-Cammell bodies which had been delivered in 1959. Both buses would pass into the fleet of West Yorkshire Passenger Transport Executive in April 1974. (Photograph B. Ridge)

June 1972, AEC Regent Vs 6210 KW, 2177 KW, 6198 KW and 6208 KW between Duties
Four of the AEC Regent Vs with H40/30F Metropolitan-Cammell bodies which had been delivered in six batches of ten to Bradford City Transport during 1963. All these buses would pass into the fleet of West Yorkshire Passenger Transport Executive in April 1974, but within eighteen months most had been sold on for further service with other operators. (Photograph B. Ridge)

July 1972, AEC Reliance OKW 106, Bradford City Centre
OKW 106 was the first of a pair of AEC Reliances with Roe B44F bodies which were new to Bradford City Transport in March 1958. They passed into the fleet of West Yorkshire Passenger Transport Executive in April 1974 but were sold for scrap very soon afterwards. (Photograph B. Ridge)

March 1973, AEC Reliance OKW 107 in Bradford

OKW 107 was the other AEC Reliance with Roe body which was new in March 1958. Both buses were used on private hire work and duplicate services. When new they were also used regularly on route 62 from Bankfoot to Buttershaw. Both were withdrawn in August 1974, a few months after the takeover by West Yorkshire PTE, and sent for scrap in October 1974. (Photograph B. Ridge)

March 1973, AEC Regent I KY 9106, Thornbury Depot

KY 9106 was an AEC Regent I with Weymann H27/24R body. It was new to Bradford Corporation in 1935, one of a batch of twenty-five. 401 was withdrawn in October 1952 but was retained to be converted into a grit wagon with a snowplough. It entered service in early 1954 as 046 and was withdrawn in 1969. It then passed into preservation. (Photograph L. Flint)

March 1973, AEC Regent III Tuition Vehicle HKW 71, Bowling Depot.
HKW 71 was an AEC Regent III 9613E built in 1952 with an East Lancashire H33/28R body. It had been part of a batch of eighteen delivered that year which were re-seated in 1957 to 35/26. To cover the shortage of buses in 1967, ten of the batch, including HKW71, were selected for overhaul rather than withdrawal and continued in service until 1972. It was then adapted to be a tuition vehicle, renumbered 037, and passed to West Yorkshire Passenger Transport Executive in April 1974. (Photograph B. Ridge)

April 1973, Daimler CVG6LX/30 EAK 239D, Bradford City Centre
Bradford 239, EAK 239D, was a Daimler CVG6LX/30 with an East Lancashire Neepsend H40/30F body. It had been new in October 1966 along with fourteen other similar vehicles, all of which were transferred to West Yorkshire PTE in April 1974. Although operated by the PTE for almost four years, none were repainted. (Photograph B. Ridge)

May 1973, AEC Regent V 6196 KW, Bradford City Centre
6196 KW was an AEC Regent V with Metropolitan-Cammell H40/30F body. It was delivered new to Bradford City Transport, in March 1964, as No. 196 in their fleet. It was part of a batch of thirty similar vehicles delivered that year which had followed sixty delivered in 1963. In April 1974 it was absorbed into the West Yorkshire PTE fleet and became 2196. This batch of vehicles was disposed of quite quickly by the PTE and some were resold for further use with other companies.

March 1974, Daimler CVG6LX/30 EAK 239D and AEC Regent V RCP 237
EAK 239D was a Daimler CVG6LX/30 with an East Lancashire Neepsend H40/30F
body. Alongside is RCP 237, which had been hired by Bradford City Transport.
It was an AEC Regent V with a Northern Counties H39/32F body that had been
new in 1962 to Hebble Motor Services. Hebble merged with Halifax Corporation in
February 1971 and RCP 237 passed to Halifax Corporation as number 76. It ran in
Halifax for a short time, but in 1972 was transferred to Calderdale Joint Omnibus
Committee and was renumbered 376 first and then 366. In April 1974, it passed to its
fourth owner, West Yorkshire Passenger Transport Executive. It was withdrawn from
service in 1976 and later purchased for preservation. It is now with the Medstead
Depot Omnibus Group in Hampshire.

March 1974, Daimler Fleetline PKW 424J, Bradford City Centre
PKW 424J was a Daimler Fleetline CRG6LX with an Alexander seventy-six-seat body,
one of forty similar vehicles delivered to Bradford Corporation Transport in 1970.
It became 2424 in the fleet of West Yorkshire PTE and was to continue in service for a
further ten years, being withdrawn in January 1985.

June 1974, Leyland PD3 LAK 311G, Bradford City Centre
LAK 311G was one of fifteen Alexander-bodied Leyland PD3s new to Bradford Corporation Transport in 1969. This batch of vehicles marked the end of an era in several ways; they were the last front-engined buses ordered by Bradford, the last half-cab bodies built by Alexander and the last Leyland Titan PD3s delivered anywhere. This bus became 2311 in the fleet of West Yorkshire PTE after April 1974 and was to continue in service for another eight years. By May 1982 it had been sold on to Walsall Council for use as a play bus.

May 1974, AEC Regents and a PD3 at Ludlam Street, Bradford
This is of the many interesting line-ups which could be seen at Ludlam Street depot, Bradford, in the 1970s. Buses from the constituent companies of the newly formed West Yorkshire PTE were gathered together, making it a half-cab haven (or maybe heaven). From left to right is Huddersfield Corporation Roe-bodied Leyland Titan PD3A/2 WVH 418, followed by four Bradford AEC Regent Vs from various batches: 2170 KW, YAK 128, 2182 KW, and YKW 161. Nearest the camera is NCX 682, of 1958 vintage, with a Roe body and still wearing the Huddersfield JOC livery, a company which had been absorbed by Huddersfield Corporation Transport in 1969.

March 1975, AEC Regent V PKY 111, Bradford City Centre
PKY 111 was an AEC Regent V with a Metropolitan-Cammell H39/31F body, one of fifteen similar vehicles delivered to Bradford City Transport in 1959. All the buses of the batch were transferred to West Yorkshire PTE in April 1974 but within a year they had been withdrawn. (Photograph B. Ridge)

June 1975, Bradford AEC Regent Vs with New Companions
This line-up of seven Bradford AEC Regent Vs front to back are 2191 KW, 2193 KW, 6215 KW, 629? KW and 6211 KW with vehicles from the fleets of Trent, Glasgow and Greater Manchester at the Paul Sykes bus sales on Wakefield Road, Barnsley. The West Yorkshire PTE quickly disposed of these newer AECs while retaining some older vehicles.

2 July 1975, Half-cab Gathering at Ludlam Street Depot, Bradford
Double-deck half-cabs from Leeds, Bradford and Huddersfield still proudly wear their former owners' livery whilst operating for West Yorkshire Passenger Transport Executive. From right to left are AEC Regent Vs 2189 KW, 2188 KW, UVH 196, Daimler CVG6LX/30s 7520 UA, 7521 UA, EAK 231D and three more AECs, including a couple of examples in the new PTE livery.

June 1976, Daimler Fleetline FKY 271E on Manningham Lane
FKY 271E was a Daimler Fleetline CRG6LX with a Metro-Cammell Weymann H43/31F body.
It had been one of a batch of fifteen vehicles delivered new to Bradford City Transport in 1967.
They passed to West Yorkshire Passenger Transport Executive in April 1974.

July 1976, AEC Swift NAK 507H in Ludlam Street Depot
NAK 507H was an AEC Swift with a Marshall B45D body, one of five similar vehicles delivered
new to Bradford City Transport in September 1969. It passed to West Yorkshire Passenger
Transport Executive in April 1974 and had been repainted by its new owners when seen
at Ludlam Street depot.

May 1977, AEC Regent V YKW 165, Little Horton Road
YKW 165 was an AEC Regent V with a Metropolitan-Cammell H40/30F body, one of sixty similar vehicles delivered new to Bradford City Transport in 1963. In April 1974 they were all taken into the fleet of West Yorkshire Passenger Transport Executive and YKW 165 was repainted in its new livery. It is seen climbing up Little Horton Road and looking rather neglected. It was in its last months of service. (Photograph B. Ridge)

May 1977, AEC Regent V 2170 KW, Bradford
2170 KW was another AEC Regent V with a Metropolitan-Cammell H40/30F body, one of a batch of sixty similar vehicles delivered new to Bradford City Transport in 1963. It became No. 2170 in the West Yorkshire Passenger Transport Executive fleet in April 1974 and is turning into Little Horton Lane, Princes Way, in its last weeks of service. (Photograph B. Ridge)

May 1977, Daimler Fleetline XAK 339L in Silver Jubilee livery
XAK 339L was a Daimler Fleetline CRL6 with an Alexander H43/31F body. It was one
of a batch of twenty similar vehicles delivered in 1972, which were to become the last new
buses delivered to Bradford City Transport before it was taken over by West Yorkshire
Passenger Transport Executive in April 1974. The Bradford district of WYPTE had XAK
339L painted in this silver and purple livery to celebrate the Queen's Silver Jubilee in 1977.
(Photograph B. Ridge)

June 1977, Daimler CVG6LX/30 EAK 227D, Bradford City Centre
EAK 227D a was a Daimler CVG6LX/30 with an East Lancashire Neepsend H40/30F
body, one of a batch of fifteen delivered to Bradford City Corporation in 1966.
They were all taken into the fleet of West Yorkshire Passenger Transport Executive
in April 1974 and were to last in service into 1978, although none received their new
owner's livery. (Photograph B. Ridge)

June 1977, Leyland PD3/2 FKY 251E, Bradford City Centre
FKY 251E was one of fifteen Leyland PD3/2s with East Lancashire Neepsend H40/30F bodies delivered new to Bradford City Transport in 1967. They were all taken into the fleet of West Yorkshire Passenger Transport Executive in April 1974 and some were repainted in the livery of their new owner. By 1978 all had been withdrawn from service, but several examples went on to work for independent operators across the country. (Photograph B. Ridge)

June 1977, Leyland PD3/2 FKY 254E, St George's Hall
FKY 254E was another of fifteen Leyland PD3/2s with East Lancashire Neepsend H40/30F bodies delivered new to Bradford City Transport in 1967. It became No. 2254 in the West Yorkshire Passenger Transport Executive fleet, although it retained its Bradford livery throughout its career. It is seen passing St George's Hall in its last months of service. (Photograph B. Ridge)

June 1977, Daimler Fleetline PKW 431J, Hall Ings
PKW 431J was a Daimler Fleetline CRG6LX with an Alexander H47/29D body, one of forty similar vehicles delivered to Bradford City Transport in 1970. All were transferred to the fleet of West Yorkshire Passenger Transport Executive in April 1974 and received new liveries during their next ten years of service. (Photograph B. Ridge)

November 1977, Daimler Fleetline XAK 348L, St George's Hall
XAK 348L was a Daimler Fleetline CRL6 with an Alexander H43/31F body, one of a batch of twenty similar vehicles delivered in 1972 to Bradford City Transport. They were taken into the fleet of West Yorkshire Passenger Transport Executive in April 1974 and eventually repainted into WYPTE colours. Only two remained in service to be part of the Yorkshire Rider fleet in 1986. (Photograph B. Ridge)

November 1977, Daimler Fleetline XAK 352L, Halifax
XAK 352L was a Daimler Fleetline CRL6. It originally had an Alexander H43/31F body, which was severely damaged after a fire in March 1974. Soon after the takeover by West Yorkshire Passenger Transport Executive it was rebodied with a low-height Northern Counties body and transferred to Halifax. It was later re-engined with a Gardner 6LXB to match the rest of the Halifax fleet. It was one of only two of this batch which were taken into the Yorkshire Rider fleet following deregulation. (Photograph B. Ridge)

April 1978, Tow Wagon 02 with Scania BR111 RYG 63R, St George's Hall
The AEC Matador towing wagon had been recently acquired by the West Yorkshire Passenger Transport Executive and worked from Todmorden. It is seen towing RYG 683R, a Scania BR111 with a Metro-Cammell-Weymann H44/31F body, which had been new in January 1977. Behind the cavalcade is LAK 319G, a Daimler Fleetline CRG6LX with an Alexander H43/31F body, new to Bradford City Transport in November 1968, edging into Ings Hall. (Photograph B. Ridge)

July 1962, Daimler CD50 CCP 606, Bulls Lane, Halifax
CCP 606 was a Daimler CD50 with an East Lancs H30/26R body. It was one of a batch of six similar vehicles delivered new to Halifax Corporation in November 1951. Daimler CD50s were unusual vehicles with powerful 10.6 litre engines and preselect gearboxes. They had hydraulic braking and steering systems which proved a very troublesome combination. They were few in numbers in Britain, most being sold abroad, with Halifax placing the largest single home order. Their mechanical problems were never satisfactorily solved by Halifax and they were sold for scrap in February 1963 after only eleven years' service. (Photograph M. Fowler)

June 1962, AEC Regent III BCP 676, Crossfields Bus Station, Halifax
BCP 676 was an AEC Regent III with a Park Royal H30/26R body, one of fourteen similar vehicles delivered new to Halifax Joint Omnibus Committee in March 1950. They were all re-seated in 1956 with three extra seats upstairs. BCP 676 was withdrawn for scrap in July 1964 and the rest of the batch had been withdrawn by 1967. BCP 671 is the one survivor, having been purchased for preservation in 1969. (Photograph M. Fowler)

June 1965, LUA 441 Farewell Tour with Halifax AEC Regent III LUA 420
LUA 420 was an AEC Regent III with a Roe H31/25R body. It was new to Leeds Corporation Transport in December 1947 and was bought by Halifax Joint Omnibus Committee from a dealer in July 1964, along with two others, to cover the late delivery of new vehicles. The bus received a partial repaint with Halifax cream over the light green of Leeds and a change of fleet number. It was finally withdrawn for scrap in December 1965. LUA 441 was a similar AEC Regent III, which, just before its withdrawal from service by Leeds, was hired by enthusiasts for a farewell tour. This tour included a visit to Halifax to meet up with some ex-Leeds AECs operated by Halifax. It has to be said that both vehicles look in remarkably good condition considering they are at the end of their careers.

September 1969, A Line-up of Halifax JOC Vehicles, Elmwood Garage
Vehicles from the fleet of Halifax Joint Omnibus Committee wait for their next duty at the back of Elmwood depot. From left to right they are: LJX 212, an AEC Regent V; PJX 234, a Leyland L1; PXO 974 and NBY 347, a pair of AEC Reliances recently rebodied by Plaxton, and finally ECP 954D, another AEC Reliance. All these buses were to be later transferred to the fleet of Calderdale Joint Omnibus Committee in September 1971. (Photograph M. Fowler)

September 1969, Dennis Loline III FCP 302E, Elmwood Garage
FCP 302E was one of the five Dennis Lolines with Northern Counties H41/33F bodies which had been delivered new to Halifax Joint Omnibus Committee in March 1967. They had many positive things in their favour but unfortunately suffered from some mechanical weaknesses. All were sold on to West Riding Automobile Company Limited of Wakefield as replacements for the ill-fated Guy Wulfrunians in early 1970. They were all withdrawn by West Riding in 1977, a mere ten years old. (Photograph M. Fowler)

June 1971, Leyland PD2/37 DCP 69D, George Street, Halifax
DCP 69D was one of seven Leyland PD2/37s with Weymann H36/28F bodies delivered new to Halifax Corporation in January 1966. The delivery had been considerably later than planned due to a lengthy industrial dispute at the Weymann works, which had made it necessary for Halifax to obtain second-hand vehicles from Leeds as a stop-gap measure. This batch of Leyland PD2s were all transferred into the fleet of West Yorkshire PTE in April 1974 and most carried their new owner's livery towards the end of the decade. DCP 69D is seen outside the Griffin Hotel on the corner of George Street and Barum Top.

June 1971, Leyland PD2/37 MCP 225, Horton Street, Halifax
MCP 225 was one of eight Leyland PD2/37 with Metropolitan-Cammell H40/32F bodies delivered new to Halifax Joint Omnibus Committee in November 1960. This batch of vehicles was transferred to the fleet of the newly formed Calderdale Joint Omnibus Committee in September 1971. MCP 225 was sold out of service in 1973 and spent some time with operators in the Home Counties before joining the fleet of Cunningham's Bus Service, Paisley, in May 1974. It is seen with its original operator turning into Horton Street, Halifax.

September 1971, Seddon Pennine RU MJX 15J, Burnley Bus Station
MJX 15J was a Seddon Pennine RU with a Plaxton Derwent DP45F body. It was one of three similar vehicles new, in late 1970, to Halifax Joint Omnibus Committee and transferred to the fleet of Calderdale Joint Omnibus Committee in September 1971. In April 1974 the three Seddons joined the fleet of the newly formed West Yorkshire PTE. MJX 15J is seen at Burnley bus station on a service from Leeds. (Photograph M. Fowler)

September 1971, Leyland Titan PD2/12s KWX 12 and KWX 14, Todmorden
KWX 12 and KWX 14 were Leyland Titan PD2/12s with Leyland L27/26R bodies. They were new to Todmorden Joint Omnibus Committee in October 1951 and had passed to the fleet of the newly formed Calderdale Joint Omnibus Committee days before this photograph was taken. Before the end of 1971 they had both been withdrawn from service and were sold on to Mulley's Motorways Limited, of Ixworth, who operated them until 1977.

March 1972, Leyland PD2 CCP 163C, Crossfields Bus Station, Halifax
CCP 163C was a Leyland PD2/7 with a Roe H37/28F body. It was one of eight similar vehicles delivered new to Halifax Corporation in September and October of 1965. These vehicles were built with teak-framed lower decks and alloy upper decks. On 1 April 1974, CCP 163C, along with the others from the same batch, was transferred to West Yorkshire PTE as fleet No. 3063 and survived in service until 1978.

June 1972, Leyland PD3/4 TCP 54, Crossfields Bus Station, Halifax

TCP 54 was one of a batch of eight Leyland PD3/4s with Weymann bodies. They were delivered to Halifax Corporation, three in December 1963, with the remainder in January 1964. All were transferred to the fleet of West Yorkshire PTE in April 1974, with TCP 54 becoming WYPTE 3054. They had only two years' service with their new operator as they were all withdrawn and scrapped in 1976.

September 1972, AEC Reliances PXO 974 and MBY 347

PXO 974 was an AEC Reliance with a Park Royal C41C and was new in April 1955 to Bourne & Balmer of Croydon. In February 1966 it became 262 in the Halifax JOC fleet. In July 1968 it was rebodied with a Plaxton Panorama I C43F body and re-entered the fleet as 257. It was transferred to the fleet of Calderdale Joint Omnibus Committee in September 1971, retaining its fleet number. It joined the West Yorkshire PTE fleet in April 1974. MBY 347 was the first of the second-hand purchases of AEC Reliances, being new to the same Croydon firm, in June 1954, and becoming 200 in the Halifax JOC fleet in July 1965. It received a new Plaxton body in October 1967 and became 256. It was eventually taken into the WYPTE fleet in April 1974. (Photograph M. Fowler)

September 1972, A Selection of Calderdale JOC Vehicles, Elmwood Garage
The formation of Calderdale Joint Omnibus Committee, in September 1971, brought together vehicles from Halifax and Todmorden JOCs, as well as some originally from Halifax Corporation. In this view there was: GJX 331, a 1956 Daimler CVG6; KWX 18, a Leyland Titan PD2/12 of 1951; PJX 45, a Leyland Titan PD2/37 of 1962 and MKH 81, a Leyland Titan PD2/12 of 1951. The latter had been purchased by Halifax as a driver training unit in November 1968 and by 1973 had been sold on for preservation. It was resold to preservationists several more times before reaching the scrapyard in 1976. Also in the group was 1881 WA, one of three Leyland Leopard L1s with ECW C41F coachwork. It was new to Sheffield Joint Omnibus Committee in 1960 and by 1970 had passed to Todmorden JOC, then Calderdale JOC, before ending its days with Aberdeen Education Department in 1977. MJX 27 was a Leyland Titan PD2/37 which had been exhibited at the Commercial Motor Show when it was new in 1960 and, finally, PJX 39, a Leyland Leopard L1 of 1962. (Photograph M. Fowler)

April 1973, Leyland RT3/1s KCP 8 and KCP 2, Skircoat Road Depot
KCP8 and KCP2 were two of a batch of nine Leyland RT3/1 Royal Tiger Worldmasters with Weymann bodies delivered in late 1958 to Halifax Corporation. KCP2 had been transferred to the Calderdale Joint Omnibus Committee in June 1972 and renumbered 372 and, in January 1974, KCP8 would follow, becoming 378. In April 1974 these two vehicles were transferred yet again, this time into the West Yorkshire PTE fleet with fleet Nos 3378 and 3372. The following year, KCP8 had found pastures new in the Republic of Ireland, while KCP2 soldiered on with WYPTE until 1979.

September 1973, Daimler SRG6LX/33 FJX 508E Heading for Halifax
FJX 508E was the last one of a batch of three Daimler SRG6LX/33s, with Willowbrook B45F bodies, delivered to Halifax Corporation in June 1967. In April 1974 all three were transferred to West Yorkshire PTE; this bus became fleet No. 3108 and was eventually repainted into the corporate livery. It continued in service until early 1981 when it was withdrawn for scrap.

September 1973, Leyland PD2/37 DCP 73D in Halifax
DCP 73D was one of eight similar Leyland PD2/37s with Weymann H36/28F bodies delivered to Halifax Corporation in January 1966. They all passed to West Yorkshire PTE in 1974. DCP 73D became 3073 and received the later WYPTE livery in 1977. At the end of its service life it became a driver training unit and was finally retired by Yorkshire Rider in 1990.

October 1973, AEC Reliance OJX 61K in Millwood Depot, Todmorden
OJX 61K was an AEC Reliance with a Plaxton Derwent II DP45F body. It was one of a pair of similar vehicles delivered new to Halifax Joint Omnibus Committee in June 1971 and passed, within three months, to the newly formed Calderdale JOC in September 1971. In April 1974 it became No. 3261 in the fleet of West Yorkshire PTE and eventually received its new livery. It is seen in Millwood depot at Todmorden next to recovery vehicle No. 402. This was an AEC Matador which had been built for the Army during the 1940s and converted for civilian use afterwards. It was No. 402 in the Halifax Corporation fleet and then R1 and 9311 with West Yorkshire PTE. It was registered as ACP 644 and was still extant in 2007, so it may well still survive.

November 1973, Daimler Fleetline BHD 222C, Skircoat Road Depot
BHD 222C had a very complicated history in terms of ownership and identity. It was an Alexander-bodied Daimler Fleetline which had been delivered new to Yorkshire Woollen District in 1965 as their No. 983 and later No. 132. In 1969 it was transferred to Hebble and became No. 350, but in March 1971 it was taken back into the Yorkshire Woollen District fleet as No. 146. Within six months of this move it had been sold to Halifax Corporation as their No. 103 and it is seen inside Skircoat Road depot in this guise. One further identity change came in April 1974 when it became 3103 in the West Yorkshire PTE fleet and eventually received a new livery. It was finally withdrawn from service in 1978.

March 1974, Leyland L1 OCP 231, Elmwood Garage
OCP 231 was a Leyland Leopard L1 with a Weymann B44F body which had been delivered new to Halifax Joint Omnibus Committee in 1961 as their fleet No. 231. The seating arrangement had been changed three times in its first three years before a satisfactory scheme was settled on. It had been delivered with a dual-door body but was converted to a front-entrance bus with forty-two seats in 1962. Two more seats were added a year later. In September 1971 this vehicle was transferred to the newly formed Calderdale Joint Omnibus Committee and, in April 1974, became 3231 in the West Yorkshire PTE fleet.

March 1974, Daimler Fleetline VCP 839M of Calderdale JOC, Bradford
VCP 839M was a Daimler Fleetline with a Northern Counties H43/31F body. It was new to Calderdale Joint Omnibus Committee in December 1973 as their 309, but within a few months (in April 1974) it became 3309 in the West Yorkshire PTE fleet. It was eventually withdrawn by Yorkshire Rider, Todmorden, in late 1988. It is seen on service in Bradford keeping company with UNW 405H, Leeds City Transport 405, which was a Leyland PDR2/1.

April 1974, AEC Reliance ECP 949D, Skircoat Road Depot, Halifax
ECP 949D was an AEC Reliance with a Pennine B39F body. It was the first of a batch of six similar vehicles delivered to Halifax Joint Omnibus Committee in late 1966. Before delivery it had been exhibited at the 1966 Commercial Motor Show. In September 1971, the six were transferred to the newly formed Calderdale Joint Omnibus Committee and, in April 1974, became 3249 in the West Yorkshire PTE fleet. It remained in service for another four years.

May 1974, AEC Reliance JCP 322F, King Street Terminus, Leeds
JCP 322F was one of a trio of AEC Reliances with Willowbrook DP41F bodies that had been delivered new to Halifax Joint Omnibus Committee in August 1968. In September 1971, they passed to Calderdale JOC and No. 262 is seen at King Street, the Leeds departure point for the service to Burnley. By the time this photograph was taken the bus had become part of the West Yorkshire PTE fleet and was soon to receive its new livery.

May 1974, Leyland Leopard UJX 918M, Halifax Bus Station
UJX 918M was a Leyland Leopard with a Plaxton Derwent B45F body which had been new
to Halifax Corporation in December. Along with the other four vehicles in this batch, it was
transferred into the fleet of West Yorkshire PTE in April 1974. Already a month into its new
ownership, it is seen entering Halifax bus station. It was later to have a standard Derwent front
end fitted after a head-on collision. It was sold for further service to Mayne's of Manchester
in 1987 and later finished its career with an independent in Pentwynmawr, Newport, in 2001.

May 1974, Leyland Titan DCP 68D, Skircoat Road Depot
DCP 68D was a Leyland Titan PD2/37 with a Weymann H36/28F body, one of a batch of
eight delivered new to Halifax Corporation in January 1966. All the vehicles passed into the
West Yorkshire PTE fleet in April 1974. Before that date a number of buses received experimental
liveries, and DCP 68D is seen in one such livery inside Skircoat Road depot. The previous year it
had received a repaint in a green and cream livery, but this was very short-lived.

September 1974, AEC Reliance ECP 949D, Skircoat Road Depot, Halifax
ECP 949D was an AEC Reliance with a Pennine B39F body, the first of seven similar vehicles
delivered to Halifax Joint Omnibus Committee in late 1966. In September 1971, along with the
other Halifax JOC vehicles, it had been transferred into the Calderdale JOC fleet. In 1973, prior
to the setting up of the West Yorkshire Passenger Transport Executive, a number of buses were
selected for repainting in various proposed liveries. ECP 949D wore one of these liveries for a
short time before receiving the adopted livery.

September 1974, NWW 89E and RCP 279K, Todmorden Bus Station
NWW 89E was one of a pair of Leyland Leopard L1s with Willowbrook B43F bodies which
were delivered to Todmorden Joint Omnibus Committee in February 1967. Another two
almost identical vehicles were purchased at the same time, but they had forty-five dual-purpose
seats. They were all to pass to the fleet of Calderdale JOC in September 1971 and then to
West Yorkshire Passenger Transport Executive in April 1974. Already wearing its new owner's
livery was RCP 279K, a Daimler Fleetline CRG6LX with a Northern Counties H43/31F body,
new to Calderdale JOC in June 1972. They await their next duties at Todmorden bus station.

October 1974, Daimler Fleetlines ECP 679D and ECP 685D, Skircoat Road Depot, Halifax
ECP 679D was the first of seven Daimler Fleetline CRG6LXs, with Northern Counties H43/31F
bodies, ordered by Halifax Corporation in late 1966. It had just received its new livery after
being transferred into the fleet of West Yorkshire Passenger Transport Executive. Behind was
ECP 685D from the same batch of buses, which had been repainted into one of the experimental
liveries tried out before the formation of the PTE.

March 1975, Leyland Titan PD2/12 KWX 17 on Driver Training Duties
KWX 17 was a Leyland Titan PD2/12 with a Leyland L27/26R body. It was new to Todmorden
Joint Omnibus Committee in October 1951 and then passed to the fleet of the newly formed
Calderdale Joint Omnibus Committee in September 1971. It later became a driver training unit
with Calderdale and, as such, joined the fleet of West Yorkshire Passenger Transport Executive
in April 1974. It continued with driver training duties until withdrawn for scrap in March 1976.

April 1975, AEC Reliance PXO 974, Leeds
PXO 974 was one of five AEC Reliances purchased second-hand by Halifax Joint Omnibus Committee from A. Timpson & Sons of Catford in 1966. It had a Park Royal C41C body and had been new, in April 1955, to Bourne & Balmer of Croydon. In February 1966 it became 262 in the Halifax fleet. In July 1968 it was rebodied with a Plaxton Panorama I C43F body and re-entered the fleet as 257. It was transferred to the fleet of Calderdale Joint Omnibus Committee in September 1971, retaining its fleet number. It joined the West Yorkshire PTE fleet in April 1974 as their 51. (Photograph B. Ridge)

April 1975, Leyland Leopard UJX 916M, Sheffield
UJX 916M was the first of five Leyland PSU4B/2Rs with Plaxton bodies delivered new to Halifax Corporation in late 1973. They were the last new vehicles to the Corporation and, along with the rest of the fleet, were transferred to West Yorkshire PTE in April 1974, UJX 916M as WYPTE 3006. It is seen at Pond Street, Sheffield, on a limited stop service to Halifax.

June 1975, Leyland Leopard JWU 254N with EJX 66D and PCP 803, Elmwood Garage
JWU 254N was a Leyland Leopard with a Plaxton Derwent body which had just been delivered
new to West Yorkshire PTE. Also at Elmwood garage was EJX 66D, an AEC Reliance with a
Willowbrook DP41F body. It had been new to Halifax Joint Omnibus Committee in November
1966 and then Calderdale JOC, before joining WYPTE in April 1974. PCP 803 was an AEC
Reliance 2MU3RA with an Alexander B43T body. It was one of a pair delivered new to Hebble
in 1962 and had passed to Halifax Corporation in April 1971. Three years later it passed to
WYPTE and was used as staff transport and finally as a driver training unit. It had just been
withdrawn when photographed and was scrapped before the end of the year.

July 1975, Leyland Leopard PSU4/4R NHE 8F, Halifax
NHE 8F was a Leyland Leopard PSU4/4R with a Marshall B45F body. It was new to Yorkshire
Traction in 1968, having been acquired by Halifax Joint Omnibus Committee, but passed
immediately to the newly formed fleet of Calderdale JOC in September 1971. It had become
part of the fleet of West Yorkshire PTE when photographed at work in Halifax.

September 1975, Leyland PD2/37s MJX 24 and MJX 26, Halifax
MJX 24 and MJX 26 were two Leyland Titan PD2/37s, with Metropolitan-Cammell H36/28F
bodies, from a batch of eight similar vehicles. They were delivered new to Halifax Corporation
in November 1960 and all eight passed to the fleet of West Yorkshire PTE in April 1974 with '30'
prefixing their original fleet numbers. By the following year these two examples were looking in
a very sorry state at the back of Elmwood garage.

April 1976, Daimler Fleetline CRG6LX VCP 837M, Cross Fields Bus Station, Halifax
VCP 837M was a Daimler Fleetline CRG6LX with a Northern Counties H43/31F body, which
had been delivered new to Calderdale Joint Omnibus Committee in December 1973. Within
months, in April 1974, it had passed to the fleet of West Yorkshire Passenger Transport Executive
as No. 3307. In October 1986 it was to join the fleet of Yorkshire Rider Limited, the successor to
the PTE, and was to continue in service for over a year. (Photograph M. Fowler)

July 1976, AEC Reliance TGJ 484
TGJ 484 was one of three 1957 AEC MU3RV Reliances, fitted with Burlingham Seagull C41F bodies, bought from A. Timpson & Sons of Catford by Halifax Joint Omnibus Committee in the summer of 1966. TGJ 484 was originally numbered 260 but was renumbered 259 the following year. In July 1968 it was rebodied with a new Plaxton Panorama I C43F body and was transferred to the fleet of the Calderdale Joint Omnibus Committee in September 1971. In April 1974 it passed to the fleet of the West Yorkshire PTE as No. 53. (Photograph B Ridge)

9 January 1977, Leyland PD2/7 CCP 165C, Todmorden Bus Station
CCP 165C was a Leyland PD2/7 with a Roe H37/28F body. It was another of the eight similar vehicles delivered new to Halifax Corporation in October of 1965. These vehicles were built with teak-framed lower decks and alloy upper decks. On 1 April 1974, CCP 165C, along with the others from the same batch, was transferred to West Yorkshire PTE. It was photographed next to the railway viaduct which overshadowed Todmorden bus station. This bus was in its final few months of service and, by October 1977, had been consigned to the scrap yard.

May 1977, Leyland PD2/37 DCP 73D, Skircoat Road Depot
DCP 73D was a Leyland Titan PD2/37 with a Weymann H36/28F body, another one of a batch of eight delivered new to Halifax Corporation in January 1966. All the vehicles passed into the West Yorkshire PTE fleet in April 1974. DCP 73D was seen at Skircoat Road depot after being repainted in the revised and simplified WYPTE livery.

June 1977, Daimler Fleetline SRG6LX KCP 423G, Halifax
KCP 423G was a Daimler Fleetline SRG6LX with a Willowbrook B45F body. It was one of three similar vehicles which had been new to new Halifax Corporation Transport in April 1969. All three were transferred into the fleet of West Yorkshire PTE in April 1974 and were soon to receive a repaint into the colours of WYPTE and in the Calderdale division.

November 1977, Daimler Fleetline JJX 597G, Halifax
JJX 597G was a Daimler Fleetline CRG6LX with a Northern Counties H43/31F body. It was one of a pair of similar vehicles delivered new to Halifax Joint Omnibus Committee in October 1968 and formed part of a batch of four, as Halifax Corporation received two identical vehicles at the same time. They were all transferred into the fleet of West Yorkshire PTE, in April 1974, and continued in service with the Calderdale division until withdrawal at the end of the decade. (Photograph B. Ridge)

March 1980, Leyland Leopard PSU4A/2R BWU 688H, Millwood Depot
BWU 688H was a Leyland Leopard PSU4A/2R with a Seddon B43F body. It was new to Todmorden Joint Omnibus Committee, in December 1969, and was the first of a batch of six vehicles delivered at the same time. It passed to the fleet of Calderdale Joint Omnibus Committee on 6 September 1971 and then on to West Yorkshire Passenger Transport Executive in April 1974. At some point, late into its career, BWU 688H had the lower front-end panel altered from the original shaped fibre glass one. Along with the other buses in this batch, it was withdrawn by 1983, but several continued in service with other operators into the 1990s.

May 1963, Karrier (Sunbeam) MS2 CVH 748, Marsden, Route 40
CVH 748 was a Karrier (Sunbeam) MS2 with an East Lancashire H40/30R body. It was the last of a batch of eight vehicles which had been delivered new to Huddersfield Corporation in August 1947. The original Park Royal body had been replaced in 1961 with the new East Lancashire body, shown in the photograph. CVH 748 remained in service until the end of Huddersfield's trolleybus system, in July 1968, and was later sold for scrap.

March 1967, BUT 9641T KVH 930, Outlane Terminus
KVH 930 was a BUT 9641T with an East Lancashire H40/32R body. It was the last of a batch of eight similar vehicles delivered new to Huddersfield Corporation in the summer of 1956 and it continued in service until the closure of the trolleybus system in July 1968. KVH 930 was seen at Outlane, the highest trolleybus terminus in the United Kingdom, before it began its return service to Waterloo.

June 1968, Sunbeam S7 PVH 931, Waterloo Terminus
PVH 931 was the last one in a batch of twelve Sunbeam S7s, with East Lancashire H40/32R bodies, which had been delivered new to Huddersfield Corporation in 1959. These vehicles were some of the very last new additions to any trolleybus system in the British Isles. It was seen leaving the Waterloo terminus in Mitchell Street on its way across the town to Outlane, which was high on the hillside overlooking Huddersfield. PVH 931 was saved from the scrapyard and is preserved by the British Trolleybus Society. It is operated regularly at the Trolleybus Museum, Sandtoft. (Photograph M. Fowler)

May 1969, AEC Reliance ACX 323A, Huddersfield
ACX 323A was the first of a pair of AEC Reliance 2MU2RAs which had been delivered new to Huddersfield Joint Omnibus Committee in December 1963. They had Roe B44F bodies, which were rather unusual owing to the addition of a driver's side cab door, which is clearly visible in this photograph. The 'A' suffix letter on the registration was also unusual because it had only been adopted by a small number of county boroughs and so very few buses were registered using this new system. They became part of the Huddersfield Corporation fleet, in October 1969, after the acquisition of the other share in the JOC. ACX 323A was later taken into the fleet of West Yorkshire PTE in April 1974.

May 1969, OCX 504F, Huddersfield
OCX 504F was a Daimler Fleetline GRG6LX with a Roe H44/31F body which was delivered new, along with fifteen others, in June 1968. All this batch of vehicles passed into the fleet of West Yorkshire PTE. OCX 504F was seen passing the newly constructed multi-storey car park and bus station, which was still five years away from opening.

June 1969, AEC Regent III HVH 238
HVH 238 was one of a batch of eight AEC Regent IIIs with East Lancashire L30/28R bodies delivered to Huddersfield Joint Omnibus Committee in October 1954. They were absorbed into the fleet of Huddersfield Corporation in October 1969 when the Corporation acquired the other share in the JOC. They remained in service until the end of 1971 with HVH 234 later preserved and HVH 239 sold for further use in the United States of America. (Photograph M. Fowler)

June 1969, Guy Arab IV PVH 990, Huddersfield

PVH 990 was a Guy Arab IV with an East Lancashire H37/28R body, one of a pair delivered new to Huddersfield Joint Omnibus Committee in 1959. They had Gardner 6LX engines and semi-automatic gearboxes which made them powerful, capable vehicles. In October 1969 they became part of the Huddersfield Corporation fleet after the Corporation had acquired the other share in the JOC, and they then passed to West Yorkshire PTE in April 1974. The second bus of the pair, PVH 991, was preserved from service, for a time after withdrawal, by WYPTE but was later sold for scrap. (Photograph M. Fowler)

October 1969, AEC Regent III FVH 174, Huddersfield

FVH 174 was an AEC Regent lll with an East Lancashire H30/28R body which had been new to Huddersfield Joint Omnibus Committee in October 1951. It was one of a batch of six vehicles which had passed to Huddersfield Corporation in October 1969, days before the photograph was taken. In February 1970, FVH 174 was sold to Telefilm Transport of Preston. The others in the batch were also soon withdrawn from service.

September 1972, Daimler CVG CCX 435B, John William Street, Huddersfield
CCX 435B was a Daimler CVG6LX-30 with an East Lancashire H39/31F body. It was the first of a batch of six vehicles delivered new to Huddersfield Corporation in November 1964. It passed into the fleet of West Yorkshire PTE in April 1974 but retained its original livery.

September 1972, Daimler Fleetline UCX 131H, John William Street, Huddersfield
UCX 131H was a Daimler Fleetline with a Roe H45/29D body. It was one of a batch of six delivered to Huddersfield Corporation in June 1970, all of which passed into the fleet of West Yorkshire PTE in April 1974.

September 1973, Leyland Titan PD2 XCX 102 with Daimler Fleetlines RCX 124G and OCX 492F, Leeds Road

XCX 102 was a Leyland Titan PD2A/24 with a Roe H37/28F body. It was new to Huddersfield Joint Omnibus Committee in 1963 and passed to Huddersfield Corporation in October 1969. It was then taken into the fleet of West Yorkshire PTE in April 1974. It was sold out of service in April 1976 and went on to be used by a local independent operator on schools contracts for a further seven years. It was seen keeping company with a pair of Huddersfield Corporation Roe-bodied Daimler Fleetlines, RCX 124G and OCX 492F, at Leeds Road football ground, the home of Huddersfield Town Football Club.

September 1973, Roe-bodied Daimler Fleetlines RCX 124G and OCX 492F, Leeds Road

OCX 492F was a Daimler Fleetline CRG6LX with a Roe H44/31F body. It was delivered new in June 1968 to Huddersfield Corporation, one of a batch of sixteen vehicles. RCX 124G was also a Roe-bodied Daimler Fleetline CRG6LX. It was one from a batch of six delivered, in February 1969, to Huddersfield Joint Omnibus Committee and passed to Huddersfield Corporation in October 1969. Their different original liveries are clearly seen as they await the return of their passengers at Leeds Road football ground, the then home of Huddersfield Town Football Club.

November 1973, NCX 687 with UVH 197 and UCX 405, Longroyd Bridge Depot
Three buses head the neat, long lines of vehicles inside Longroyd Bridge depot, Huddersfield. NCX 687 was an AEC Regent V with a Roe H37/28R body, new to Huddersfield Joint Omnibus Committee in March 1958. UVH 197 was an AEC Regent V with a Roe H39/31F body. It was new in January 1962 to Huddersfield Joint Omnibus Committee and passed to Huddersfield Corporation in October 1969. UCX 405 was a Leyland Titan PD3A/2 with a Roe H39/31F body, new in November 1961 to Huddersfield Corporation. Works vehicle A5, MCX 24F, was an Austin A60 van.

November 1973, AEC Regents UVH 198, UVH 201 and JVH 379, Longroyd Bridge Depot
UVH 198 and UVH 201 were AEC Regent Vs with Roe H39/31F bodies. They had been new to Huddersfield Joint Omnibus Committee in January 1962 and passed to Huddersfield Corporation in October 1969. JVH 379 was a 1955 AEC Regent III with an East Lancashire H33/28R body, also new to Huddersfield Joint Omnibus Committee. They were positioned over the inspection pits in Longroyd Bridge depot.

November 1973, AEC Regent ECX 425, Longroyd Bridge Depot

ECX 425 was an AEC Regent lll with a Northern Coachbuilders L29/26R body. It was delivered new, in July 1949, to Huddersfield Joint Omnibus Committee and passed to Huddersfield Corporation in October 1969. It was used as as a driver training unit by Huddersfield and was transferred into the fleet of West Yorkshire PTE. After retirement from its driver training duties in 1975, the vehicle was preserved and is currently under restoration at the Keighley Bus Museum.

February 1974, OCX 502F, Oldham
OCX 502F was one of a batch of sixteen Daimler Fleetline CRG6LXs with a
Roe H44/31F bodies. It was delivered new in June 1968 to Huddersfield Corporation
and became part of the fleet of West Yorkshire PTE within weeks of the photograph.
It eventually received the livery of its new owners and continued in service into the 1980s.

March 1974, Daimler CVG6LXs 7504 UA and HVH 465D, Manchester Street
Bus Station
7504 UA was a Daimler CVG6LX.30DD with a Roe H39/32R body and one of a
batch of thirty buses delivered to Leeds City Transport in October 1959. HVH
465D was also a Daimler CVG6LX-30 but with an East Lancashire H41/29F body.
Both vehicles were transferred to the West Yorkshire PTE fleet, but 7504 UA had an
open platform and rear entrance, making it an early candidate for withdrawal in 1976.

March 1974, JVN 379, UVH98 and UCX 408, Longroyd Bridge Depot, Huddersfield
UCX 408 was a Leyland Titan PD3A/2 with a Roe H39/31F body, new in November 1961 to Huddersfield Corporation. UVH 198 was an AEC Regent V with Roe H39/31F body. It had been new to Huddersfield Joint Omnibus Committee in January 1962 and passed to Huddersfield Corporation in October 1969. JVH 379 was a 1955 AEC Regent III with an East Lancashire H33/28R body, also new to Huddersfield Joint Omnibus Committee. All three buses were days away from becoming part of the fleet of West Yorkshire PTE in April 1974, but all were withdrawn before the end of the decade.

April 1974, Leyland Titan PD3A/2 WVH 418, Ludlam Street Depot
WVH 418 was a Leyland Titan PD3A/2 Roe H39/31F body. It was new to Huddersfield Corporation in January 1963 and the penultimate delivery in a batch of ten similar vehicles, which replaced trolleybuses on the Marsden route. From January 1974 it had been on hire to Bradford City Transport at Ludlam Street depot, and it remained there for some time after the takeover by West Yorkshire PTE. Eventually it was transferred to the Halifax district and repainted in the corporate livery. It remained in service until late 1979.

June 1974, Daimler CVG6LX DCX 112B, Huddersfield
DCX 112B was a Daimler CVG6LXDD with a Roe H37/28F body. It had been one of a batch of six delivered new to Huddersfield Joint Omnibus Committee in November 1964 and passed to Huddersfield Corporation in October 1969. By the time of this photograph, it had become part of the fleet of West Yorkshire PTE and had the number four added to the front of its fleet number.

July 1974, AEC Regents UVH 199, NCX 683, UVH 200, NCX 689 and YAK 127, Ludlam Street Depot
After the formation of West Yorkshire Passenger Transport Executive and the setting up of the four districts, an effort was made to standardise vehicle types to different districts. Bradford became the home of the AEC Regents and this photograph at Ludlam Street depot illustrates this with YAK 127, an AEC Regent V with Metropolitan-Cammell H39/31F body which had been delivered to Bradford Corporation Transport in November 1962. NCX 689 and NCX 683 were exposed radiator AEC Regent Vs with Roe H37/28R bodies, new in March 1958 to Huddersfield Joint Omnibus Committee. Finally, freshly repainted UVH 199 and UVH 200 were AEC Regent Vs with Roe H39/31F bodies which were from a batch of six, new to Huddersfield Joint Omnibus Committee in January 1962.

8 September 1974, AEC Regents, Ludlam Street
Fourteen former Huddersfield Corporation and Bradford City Transport AEC Regent Vs make an impressive line-up after inter-district transfer to Ludlam Street depot. The standardisation of vehicle types to the various districts of the newly formed West Yorkshire PTE was a very practical solution to concentrate repairs, spare parts and expertise to increase efficiency.

8 September 1974, AEC Regent V NCX 682, Ludlam Street Depot, Bradford
NCX 682 was an AEC Regent V with a Roe H37/28R body, new to Huddersfield Joint Omnibus Committee in March 1958, and passed to Huddersfield Corporation in October 1969. It became part of the fleet of West Yorkshire PTE in April 1974 and was transferred to Ludham Street depot, Bradford, along with other Huddersfield AEC Regents.

September 1974, AEC Reliance SCX 20, Huddersfield
SCX 20 was an AEC Reliance with a Roe B44F body. It had been delivered new to Huddersfield Joint Omnibus Committee in October 1960 and transferred into the Huddersfield Corporation fleet in October 1969. Its final change of ownership came in April 1974 with the formation of West Yorkshire Passenger Transport Executive. It was withdrawn in early 1976 without receiving a repaint into the new WYPTE livery.

September 1974, Seddon Pennine UCX 239H, Longroyd Bridge Depot, Huddersfield
UCX 239H was a Seddon Pennine with a Pennine RU B43D body which had been converted to one-door B45F in July 1973. It was the last of a batch of six which had been delivered to Huddersfield Corporation Transport in August 1970 and became part of the fleet of West Yorkshire PTE in April 1974. It eventually received the livery of its new owners.

October 1974, Daimler CVG6LX/30DD CCX 439B at the Terminus
CCX 439B was a Daimler CVG6LX/30DD with an East Lancashire H39/31F body. It was the last in a batch of six buses delivered to Huddersfield Corporation Transport, in November 1964, and passed to the fleet of West Yorkshire PTE in April 1974.

June 1975, Daimler CVG6LX30 AVH 431B, Longroyd Bridge Depot
At the head of a line of similar buses was AVH 431B, a Daimler CVG6LX/30DD with a Roe H39/31F body. It was one of a batch of ten buses new to Huddersfield Corporation in February 1964 and was taken into the fleet of West Yorkshire PTE in April 1974.

31 January 1976, Guy Arab IV 6LX PVH 991, Longroyd Bridge Depot
PVH 991 was one of a pair of Guy Arab IVs with Gardner 6LX engines, semi-automatic gearboxes and East Lancashire H37/28R bodies. They were new to Huddersfield Joint Omnibus Committee in October 1959 and passed to Huddersfield Corporation in October 1969. PVH 991 was taken into the fleet of West Yorkshire PTE in April 1974. It was retired later in 1976 and was bought for preservation. Unfortunately, it suffered vandal damage and was scrapped.

February 1976, Leyland PD3 UCX 403, near Hard End
UCX 403 was a Leyland PD3A/2 with a Roe H39/31F body which was new, in November 1961, to Huddersfield Corporation Transport. It was transferred to the fleet of West Yorkshire PTE as 4403. It is seen climbing gradually while on service 50 from Huddersfield to Marsden Hard End. It was an aptly named destination on a bitterly cold day at this isolated terminus.

February 1976, AEC Regent V PVH 992, Slaithwaite
PVH 992 was an AEC Regent V 2D2RA with East Lancashire H37/28R body. It was the first of a pair of similar vehicles delivered new to Huddersfield Joint Omnibus Committee, in February 1960, with the fleet No. 192. In October 1969 the routes and vehicles of the JOC, including PVH 992, were absorbed by Huddersfield Corporation Transport. The AEC was still part of the fleet at the takeover by West Yorkshire PTE in April 1974. It is seen at the Slaithwaite turning circle a short time before its withdrawal.

February 1976, Daimler CVG6LX EVH 119C, Slaithwaite
EVH 119C was one of a batch of six Daimler CVG6LX-30s with Roe H39/31F bodies delivered in October 1965 to Huddersfield Joint Omnibus Committee. In October 1969 it was absorbed into the fleet of Huddersfield Corporation Transport. It became 4119 in the fleet of West Yorkshire PTE in April 1974 and received the new livery quite quickly. It was photographed in the former trolleybus turning circle at Slaithwaite.

February 1976, Leyland PD3A UCX 403 at Marsden Hard End Terminus.
UCX 403 was one of eight similar Leyland PD3A/2s with Roe H39/31F bodies, which were new in November 1961 to Huddersfield Corporation Transport. It became part of the WYPTE fleet as 4403 and is photographed at the terminus named Marsden Mount Road, Hard End, on the northern edge of the Peak District.

February 1976, Daimler Fleetline RVH 464N, Marsden, Hard End Terminus
RVH 464N was a Daimler Fleetline CRG6LX with Roe H44/31F body, delivered in August 1974 to West Yorkshire PTE as 4164. It had been part of an order for seventeen similar vehicles placed by Huddersfield Corporation Transport before its demise in April 1974. In October 1986 it was absorbed into the Yorkshire Rider fleet and, although it received a new livery, was scrapped by August 1988. It was photographed working Route 52, waiting at the terminus named Marsden Mount Road, Hard End, on the northern edge of the Peak District.

March 1976, Daimler CRG6LX KVH 485E, John William Street, Huddersfield
KVH 485E was one of sixteen Daimler CRG6LXs with Roe H44/31F bodies delivered to Huddersfield Corporation Transport in July 1967. In April 1974 it became 4485 in the West Yorkshire PTE fleet and received the new livery shortly afterwards. KVH 485E is seen on service in John William Street, Huddersfield, with the wonderful art deco shop in the background.

March 1976, Leyland PD3A/2 WVH 412, Halifax Crossfields Bus Station
WVH 412 was a Leyland PD3A/2 with a Roe H39/31F body that had been delivered new in October 1962. It was one of a batch of sixteen similar vehicles ordered by Huddersfield Corporation Transport as trolleybus replacements. In April 1974 it was absorbed into the fleet of West Yorkshire PTE as 4412 and transferred to work out of Halifax. It quickly received the new livery but by July 1978 it had been withdrawn from service.

March 1976, CCX 435B with KVH 482E, John William Street
CCX 435B was a Daimler CVG6LX-30 with an East Lancashire H39/31F body. It was new to Huddersfield Corporation Transport in November 1964, the first of a batch of six similar vehicles. It passed into the fleet of West Yorkshire PTE in April 1974. KVH 482E was a Daimler Fleetline CRG6 with a Roe H43/32F body, one of sixteen delivered to Huddersfield Corporation in July 1967. It was equipped with a door to close off the upper saloon and was later converted to one-man operation. It passed into the fleet of West Yorkshire PTE in April 1974 and was quickly repainted into its new owner's livery. (Photograph M. Fowler)

September 1976, AEC Regent V ENW 974D and Leyland PD3A2 UCX 403, Bramley Garage
ENW 974D was an AEC Regent V with a Roe H39/31R body. It had been new to Leeds City Transport in January 1966. Next to it is UCX 403, a Leyland PD3A/2 with a Roe H39/31F body which had been new in November 1961 to Huddersfield Corporation Transport. Along with other withdrawn vehicles, they await disposal from Bramley Garage.

April 1977, Daimler Fleetline RVH 463N Commemorating the Silver Jubilee
RVN 463N was a Daimler Fleetline CRG6LX with a Roe H44/31F body. It was one of a batch of similar vehicles ordered by Huddersfield Corporation but delivered in August 1974, some four months after the formation of West Yorkshire PTE. It was chosen to be one of the four buses repainted in a special livery to commemorate the Queen's Silver Jubilee. A full load of eager passengers await departure as the driver checks the runners and riders for the 2:30 at Chepstow.

June 1979, AEC Regent V NCX 686, Driver Training Duties
NCX 686 was one of eight AEC Regent Vs with Roe H37/28R bodies which had been delivered new to Huddersfield Joint Omnibus Committee, in March 1958, and passed to Huddersfield Corporation in October 1969. NCX 686 became part of the fleet of West Yorkshire PTE, in April 1974, and was transferred to Bradford along with other Huddersfield AEC Regents. It was converted as a driver training unit after withdrawal from normal service.

June 1981, Daimler CRG6LX KVH 473E, Westgate, Huddersfield
KVH 473E was the first of a batch of sixteen Daimler CRG6LXs with Roe H44/31F bodies delivered to Huddersfield Corporation Transport in July 1967. These were the vehicles that ended the tradition of the classic half-cab double-deck buses which had graced the streets of Huddersfield. KVH 473E was transferred into the fleet of West Yorkshire PTE in April 1974 and remained in service for another ten years. It is seen in Huddersfield in the final simplified WYPTE livery which had been adopted as standard. It is now preserved in working order by the Keighley Bus Museum Trust.

16 July 1963, Leeds City Transport Leyland NNW 341, Swinnow House Terminus
NNW 341 was a Leyland PD2/1 with a Leyland H30/26R body, new in December 1949 to Leeds City Transport as their No. 341. It was one of a large batch of sixty buses of this type, which were delivered new to Leeds City Transport at the end of 1949 and early in 1950, and would remain in service for another year after this photograph, being withdrawn in June 1964. It is seen in the newly constructed Swinnow House Terminus at one end of the No. 11 route to Gipton.

10 August 1963, AEC Regent V WUA 839, Leeds City Station
WUA 839 was a 1956 AEC Regent V with a Roe H33/27R body, new to Leeds City Transport. It is easily identified even though the registration plate and fleet number are obscured by the crew because of its gold lining on the upper body. This was applied by Roe who used the bus as their exhibit at the 1956 Commercial Motor Show in Earl's Court. The bus is standing at Leeds City railway station during a period of reconstruction of the area.

1 September 1963, Daimler CVG6LX 7516 UA, New Market Street
7516 UA was a Daimler CVG6LX.30DD with a Roe H39/32R body and one of a batch of thirty buses delivered to Leeds City Transport, in October 1959, as tramway replacement vehicles. In April 1974 it joined the fleet of West Yorkshire PTE, but its working life was cut short because it had a rear entrance with an open platform. It was seen working service 14 in New Market Street.

14 September 1963, AEC Regent III TNW 759, Briggate
TNW 759 was an AEC Regent III with a Metropolitan-Cammell H33/25R body. It was new in December 1954 to Leeds City Transport and the last in a batch of five similar vehicles. TNW 759 was unique in the batch because it was fitted with a fluid flywheel which made it difficult to make smooth gear changes. It was to remain in service until the middle of 1970, after which it was dispatched to the scrapyard.

15 March 1964, AEC Regent V XUM 855, Temple Newsam
XUM 855 was an AEC Regent V with a Roe H33/27R body. It was delivered new in October 1957 to Leeds City Transport, one of a batch of fifty-five similar vehicles. It was seen at Temple Newsam before departing back to the city centre during a heavy fall of snow.

June 1964, Leyland Titans 315 DUA, 5227 NW and NNW 384, Leeds
Three generations of Leyland Titans in service with Leeds City Transport. 315 DUA was a
Leyland Titan PD3A/2 with Weymann H39/31R bodywork. It was new to Leeds City Transport
in 1962 as their No. 315. 5227 NW was a Leyland Titan PD3/5 with a Roe H39/32R body, new
to Leeds City Transport in March 1959 as their No. 227. NNW 384 was a Leyland Titan PD2/1
with a Leyland H30/26R body, new in 1950 as Leeds City Transport's No. 364.

June 1964, AEC Reliance 8738 UA, Sovereign Street Bus Depot
8738 UA was an AEC Reliance with a Roe B34C body. It was one of a pair which was
delivered new, in November 1959, to Leeds City Transport. It awaits its next turn of duty at
Leeds Sovereign Street bus depot.

June 1964, AEC Regent III LUA 446, Leeds Central Bus Station
LUA 446 was an AEC Regent III with Roe H31/25R body. It was delivered new to Leeds City Transport in 1948, one of a batch of nineteen similar vehicles. The bodies on this batch were unusual because they did not have the Roe 'trademark' waist-rail. Although looking in excellent external condition, LUA 446 was at the end of its career, being withdrawn in early 1965. The car showroom in the background, on Duke Street, has a brand-new Austin A40 and a Mini Traveller for sale, along with some foreign competition in the shape of a Simca.

July 1964, AEC Regent V WUA 839, Elland Road
Here is another photograph of WUA 839, a 1956 AEC Regent V with a Roe H33/27R body. It had been a show bus for Roe at the 1956 Commercial Motor Show in Earl's Court, hence its gold lining. The location is interesting, with Elland Road, home of Leeds United, in the background. The date is also significant for the football club because they had just been promoted into the First Division of the Football League (the top division in those days) and were a few weeks away from their first game of the new season.

July 1964, Daimler CVG6 VUG 536 Heads around the Eastgate Roundabout
VUG 536 was a Daimler CVG6 with a Metropolitan-Cammell H33/28R body. It was one of a batch of twenty similar vehicles delivered new to Leeds City Transport in early 1956. It was photographed negotiating the Eastgate roundabout with Appleyard's petrol filling station in the centre of it. Behind the bus are the Quarry Hill Flats; they were the largest social housing complex in the United Kingdom and were demolished in 1978. In the middle background is Tetley's Brewery, another Leeds landmark, which was demolished in 2012.

August 1964, AEC Regent III TNW 730, Leeds Central Bus Station
TNW 730 was an AEC Regent III with a Roe H33/25R body. It was the first of a batch of thirty similar vehicles delivered new, in July 1954, to Leeds City Transport and had been exhibited at the 1954 Commercial Motor Show. Ten years later it had received a repaint and lost the gold leaf lining from its exhibition appearance. It was to remain in service for another seven years.

April 1965, AEC Regent III ONW 627, Infirmary Street
ONW 627 was an AEC Regent III with a Roe H31/25R body. It was one of twenty-three, in what was the first batch of twenty-three 8-foot-wide buses, delivered new in January 1951. Leeds City Transport did not allow these buses to operate on routes into the bus station because of their width and no more 8-foot buses were ordered until 1958. The bus station was rebuilt with wider lanes in 1963 which allowed the use of all width vehicles. This batch of buses was gradually withdrawn from service by the end of 1969. It was photographed on Infirmary Street with a Bradford City Transport AEC Regent III just behind.

August 1965, Daimler CVG6LX 572 CNW, Westgate Roundabout
572 CNW was a Daimler CVG6LX with Roe H39/31F body. It was new, in May 1962, to Leeds City Transport and was one of a batch of five front-entrance Daimlers. All five buses were transferred to the fleet of West Yorkshire PTE in April 1974. In the following months they were transferred to Kirklees District and eventually to Calderdale District, in December 1975. 572 CNW was withdrawn in 1977 and was transferred to West Yorkshire Metropolitan County Council as a mobile exhibition unit. It then passed to the West Yorkshire Transport Museum for preservation and was sold to the Quantock Motor Services heritage fleet. It was exported to Italy in 2011 and is now at Lido di Venice as an El Pecador food outlet.

May 1966, AEC Reliance 45 KUA, Old Bramley Depot
45 KUA was an AEC Reliance with a Roe B41D body. It was the second of four similar vehicles delivered new to Leeds City Transport, in August 1964, and is seen here outside the old Bramley garage, which was formerly Bramley tram depot. All four buses were sold by Leeds, after only eight years, to Aberdeen Corporation, in 1971, for use on their inaugural one-man-operation service. 45 KUA and at least two of the others passed to Wilsons of Carnwath in 1977 and worked for them for a further six years.

August 1966, Leyland PD2/1 NNW 397 with AEC Regent III NNW 493, Eastgate
NNW 397 was an all-Leyland PD2/1 with H30/26R body. It was one of a large batch of sixty buses of this type which were delivered new to Leeds City Transport at the end of 1949 and early 1950. NNW 493 was a 1950 AEC Regent III with a Roe H31/25R body, one of a batch of twenty-five. Both buses were coming to the end of their careers and would not be in service with Leeds by the end of the decade.

May 1967, AEC Regent III NNW 483 Negotiating the Eastgate Roundabout
NNW 483 was another AEC Regent III, with a Roe H31/25R body, from a batch of twenty-five
delivered new to Leeds City Transport in 1950. It was photographed heading round the Eastgate
roundabout with the Quarry Hill Flats in the background. The size of this housing complex,
opened in 1938, is clearly visible but within twelve years it would be swept away. NNW 483,
although appearing to be in excellent condition, was in its last months of service.

July 1967, AEC Regent III NUM 700 Passing the Changing Leeds Skyline
NUM 700 was an AEC Regent III with a Roe H31/25R body. It was the Roe exhibit at the
1950 Commercial Motor Show and was the second 8-foot-wide vehicle in the Leeds City
Transport fleet. It entered service in November 1950 and continued to operate in Leeds until
July 1969.

July 1967, Daimler CVG6 YNW 560 Heading out of Leeds
YNW 560 was a Daimler CVG6 with a Metropolitan-Cammell-Weymann H33/27R body. It was one of a batch of twenty similar vehicles delivered new to Leeds City Transport, in September 1957, as tram replacements on the Dewsbury Road to Moortown and Roundhay route. It had recently received a repaint and looked immaculate as it headed out of the city on a very quiet road.

July 1967, Leyland Atlantean HUA 354D, The Mint, Holbeck
HUA 354D was a Leyland Atlantean with a Metropolitan-Cammell-Weymann H41/29F body. It was the penultimate vehicle in a batch of fifteen which were delivered new to Leeds City Transport in January. They were the last 30-foot buses ordered by Leeds and all were taken into the fleet of West Yorkshire PTE in April 1974. Bradford seems to have become their last refuge but most of them had been withdrawn by 1978. At least one soldiered on until June 1980. HUA 354D was about six months old when photographed on Service 52 to Morley. The long demolished CWS menswear clothing factory at The Mint, Holbeck, is in the background.

October 1967, Leyland Tiger Cub TUA 29 Heads over the Cobbles
TUA 29 was a Leyland Tiger Cub PSUC1/1 with a Roe B34+24C standee body. It was one of a trio of similar vehicles which had been delivered new to Leeds City Transport, in March 1955, in a strategy to combine high passenger capacity with a low-height, low-weight vehicle. The buses operated on routes with low and weak bridges but were particularly unpopular with the many passengers who had to stand up. One of the three, TUA 31, remained for many years in a scrapyard and attempts were made to preserve it.

May 1968, Daimler CVG6 VUG 540, Wellington Street
VUG 540 was a Daimler CVG6 with a Metropolitan-Cammell H33/28R body. It was one of a batch of twenty delivered new to Leeds City Transport, in January 1956, as tram replacements for the Lawnswood to Beeston route. Looking immaculate after a recent overhaul and repaint, it was photographed picking up passengers in Wellington Street.

July 1968, AEC Regent III MUG 466, Leeds Central Bus Station
MUG 466 was an AEC Regent III with a Roe H31/25R body. It was one of twenty-five similar vehicles delivered new to Leeds City Transport in September 1949. These were the first buses to feature the waist-rail around the lower body, a detail which became a trademark of the Roe bodywork. Most of this batch of vehicles had been withdrawn by the time of the photograph and MUG 466, which was working an enthusiast's special, would quickly follow them to the scrapyard.

February 1969, AEC Regent III NUB 616, Leeds Central Bus Station
NUB 616 was an AEC Regent III with a Roe H31/25R body. It was one in a batch of twenty-five delivered new to Leeds City Transport in the summer of 1950. They were the last new buses delivered in the old blue livery, which was replaced by the classic two shades of green. NUB 616 was in its last year of service and the weather conditions on the day of the photograph were certainly not conducive to shiny, clean vehicles, yet there is still an air of purposeful elegance about the bus.

May 1970, Daimler CVG6 YNW 563, Boar Lane
YNW 563 was a Daimler CVG6 with a Metropolitan-Cammell-Weymann H33/27R body.
It was one of a batch of twenty similar vehicles which had been new to Leeds City Transport
in 1957 as tram replacements. It was seen working along Boar Lane on a service to Bramley.
All twenty of the buses in this batch had been withdrawn by early 1972.

8 September 1971, AEC Regent V 1908 NW, Boar Lane
1908 NW was an AEC Regent V with a Roe H33/29R body. It was one of fifteen delivered
in July 1958 to Leeds City Transport, particularly for use on service 1 Lawnswood to Beeston.
They were not particularly long-lived as they had all been withdrawn before the West Yorkshire
PTE takeover in April 1974.

October 1971, MUB 191F with UNW 210H near Leeds Central Bus Station
MUB 191F was an AEC Swift with Metropolitan-Cammell-Weymann B48D body. It was delivered new, in May 1968, in a batch of thirty vehicles and they passed into the fleet of West Yorkshire PTE in April 1974. UNW 210H was a Daimler Fleetline with a Park Royal B48D body. It was one of thirty similar buses delivered to Leeds City Transport in February 1970. All of these passed into the fleet of West Yorkshire PTE, some giving another ten years of service before withdrawal.

November 1971, Leyland Atlantean UNW 403H, Leeds Central Bus Station
UNW 403H was a Leyland Atlantean PDR2/1 with a Roe H45/33D body. It was one of fifteen Atlaneans new to Leeds City Transport in January 1970. It passed into the fleet of West Yorkshire PTE in April 1974 and was sold out of service to Ipswich Borough Transport in 1980. It was one of four bought from this batch to go there. After its time with Ipswich, in 1986 UNW 403H was preserved and, in the late 1990s, it was exported for use in France by La Ferme du Buisson Dance and Theatre Company in Noisiel.

26 March 1972, Daimler CVG6 516 CNW, Wellington Street
516 CNW was a 1962 Daimler CVG6 with a Roe H39/31F body. It was one of a batch of five front-entrance Daimlers ordered by Leeds City Transport, which passed to West Yorkshire PTE in April 1974. The batch were eventually transferred to Calderdale District in December 1975. This was as part of the executive's attempt to standardise vehicle types to the various districts in order to concentrate repairs, spare parts and expertise in one depot.

May 1972, 1959 Daimler CVG6LX/30 7503 UA and ANW 446J, City Square
7503 UA was another of the Daimler CVG6LX/30DDs, with a Roe H39/32R body, from the batch of thirty buses delivered to Leeds City Transport, in October 1959, as tramway replacement vehicles. ANW 446J was a Leyland Atlantean PDR2/1 with a Roe H45/33D body. It was new to Leeds City Transport in February 1971, the first of twenty similar vehicles. Both of these buses passed into the fleet of West Yorkshire PTE in April 1974. The Daimler was withdrawn within twelve months but the Atlantean lasted until November 1982.

27 May 1972, Daimler Fleetline CRG6LX 109 LNW, Leeds City Centre
109 LNW was a Daimler Fleetline CRG6LX with a Roe H41/29F body. It was the penultimate vehicle in a batch of ten delivered to Leeds City Transport in December 1964, the first rear-engine buses for Leeds. In April 1974 it passed into the fleet of West Yorkshire PTE, but was not repainted into the PTE livery, being withdrawn in early 1977. The first five buses in the batch were transferred to the Calderdale division in 1974 and lasted in service much longer, one until the summer of 1982.

July 1972, DUA 466K, PNW 363G and 3911 UB, Leeds Central Bus Station
DUA 466K, nearest the camera, was a Leyland Atlantean PDR2/1 with a Roe H45/33D body. It was one of thirty similar buses delivered to Leeds City Transport, in July 1971, and passed to West Yorkshire PTE in April 1974. It eventually passed into the fleet of the PTE's successor, Yorkshire Rider, being withdrawn in 1987. PNW 363G, in the middle, was a Leyland Atlantean PDR2/1 with a Park Royal H45/33F body, also from a batch of thirty delivered in September 1968. It would work for West Yorkshire PTE into 1981. Finally, 3911 UB was an AEC Regent V with a Metropolitan-Cammell-Weymann Orion H39/32R body which had been delivered in May 1960. It also passed to West Yorkshire PTE in April 1974 but was withdrawn within twelve months.

October 1972, AEC Regent V 3912 UB, Sovereign Street Depot
3912 UB was an AEC Regent V with a Metropolitan-Cammell-Weymann Orion H39/32R body which had been delivered in May 1960. It was one of fourteen similar buses which formed the last batch of exposed radiator vehicles purchased by Leeds City Transport. It was taken into the fleet of West Yorkshire PTE in April 1974 but was withdrawn shortly afterwards. It was seen pulling away from a line of parked buses in Sovereign Street depot.

October 1972, AEC Regent JUM 220L with WUA 770 and WUA 775, Sovereign Street Depot
JUM 220L was a brand-new Daimler Fleetline with a Roe H45/33D body. It had been delivered, days before the photograph was taken, to Leeds City Transport, one of a batch of thirty similar buses. They were to be taken into the fleet of West Yorkshire PTE in April 1974, with withdrawals taking place mainly in 1985. WUA 770 and WUA 775 were AEC Regent Vs with Roe H33/27R bodies. They were part of a large batch of eighty similar buses delivered new to Leeds City Transport throughout 1956.

March 1973, Daimler Fleetline CRG6LX FUB 116D, Ludlam Street Depot, Bradford
FUB 116D was the first of fifteen Daimler Fleetline CRG6LXs with Roe H41/29F bodies which
had been delivered new to Leeds City Transport in May 1966. They all went into the fleet of
West Yorkshire PTE at the takeover in April 1974. Twelve of the batch were withdrawn in 1976,
when only ten years old, but FUB 116D soldiered on and was finally withdrawn from service in
August 1983. It was seen in Bradford, having worked the joint 78 Leeds to Bradford route that
had been taken over, in 1967, from Samuel Ledgard by Leeds.

April 1973, AEC Regent V 3923 UB, Corn Exchange
3923 UB was an AEC Regent V with a Metropolitan-Cammell-Weymann Orion H39/32R body
which had been delivered in May 1960. This bus was the last vehicle with an exposed radiator
to be purchased by Leeds City Transport. It was taken into the fleet of West Yorkshire PTE in
April 1974 but was withdrawn within twelve months.

April 1973, Leyland PD3/5 5274 NW, Corn Exchange
5274 NW was a Leyland Titan PD3/5 with Roe H38/32R bodywork. It was one of a batch
of thirty which were delivered to Leeds City Transport in March 1959. Withdrawals of some
members of the batch began in 1973 but a number of these buses were taken into the fleet of
West Yorkshire PTE in April 1974. None of them lasted long enough to receive a repaint into the
PTE livery. However, a number of them went on to work for other operators.

April 1973, MNW 167F, Leeds Central Bus Station
MNW 167F was an AEC Swift with a Metropolitan-Cammell-Weymann B48D body. It was
one of a batch of thirty similar buses new to Leeds City Transport in April 1968. It was painted
in the reversed livery to denote one-man operated buses. All of the buses in this batch were
transferred into the fleet of West Yorkshire PTE in April 1974.

August 1973, Daimler Fleetline UNW 217H, West Yorkshire Road Car Depot, Leeds
UNW 217H was a Daimler Fleetline with a Park Royal B48D body. It had been delivered to
Leeds City Transport in 1970, one of a batch of thirty similar vehicles. They were to pass to the
fleet of West Yorkshire PTE in April 1974, with the first of the batch being withdrawn in 1980.
The rest were all gone by 1984. It is seen outside the West Yorkshire Road Car Company depot
in Leeds while on an enthusiast's tour of the area.

12 January 1974, A Line-up at Sovereign Street Depot
SUB 412G was an AEC Swift with a Park Royal B48D body, UNW 210H was a Daimler
Fleetline with a Park Royal B48D body, 946 GUA was an AEC Regent V with a Roe H39/31R
body, SUG 567M was a Leyland Atlantean with a Roe H45/33D body and 593 FUM was a
Daimler CVG6LX/30 with a Roe H39/31R body. All were new to Leeds City Transport and
within three months of this photograph all would be taken into the fleet of West Yorkshire
Passenger Transport Executive.

August 1974, AEC Regent V DUM 971C, Leeds Central Bus Station
DUM 971C was an AEC Regent V with a Roe H39/31R body. It was one of a batch of ten that had been delivered new, in December 1965, to Leeds City Transport. Another ten were to follow early in 1966, which were the last rear-entrance buses ordered by Leeds. They had all become part of the fleet of West Yorkshire PTE in April 1974. Although DUM 971C looked to be in fine fettle when seen on service at the Central bus station, its new owners would dispose of it within twelve months.

May 1975, Daimler CVG6 574 CNW Leaves Halifax Bus Station en Route for Huddersfield
574 CNW was a Daimler CVG6LX with Roe H39/31F body. It was new in May 1962 to Leeds City Transport and was one of a batch of five front-entrance Daimlers. It passed into the fleet of West Yorkshire PTE in April 1974 and was transferred first to Kirklees and then Calderdale District along with other Daimlers. After its service life was over, it was selected for transfer to the West Yorkshire County Council for conversion to an exhibition bus. 574 CNW has survived into preservation and can still be seen working in the streets of West Yorkshire. Wearing its West Yorkshire PTE livery well, it is seen leaving Halifax bus station en route for Huddersfield.

May 1975, Leyland PDR2/1 Atlantean PNW 357G, Bradford
PNW 357G was a Leyland Atlantean with a Park Royal H45/33F body. It was delivered new in September 1968 to Leeds City Transport, one in a batch of thirty. They were the only substantial batch of Park Royal-bodied vehicles delivered to Leeds and also represented the last of a number of features common to Leeds buses. They were the last Leeds buses delivered in the old-style green livery, the last one-door double-deck buses and the last to carry the illuminated limited stop sign at the front. The whole batch were transferred to the fleet of West Yorkshire PTE in April 1974 and most moved to other districts away from Leeds. They were all withdrawn by 1981 and scrapped.

April 1976, Leyland Atlantean HWT 38N, Sovereign Street Depot
HWT 38N was a Leyland Atlantean with a Roe H43/33F body. It was one of a batch of forty similar vehicles delivered in early 1975 to West Yorkshire Passenger Transport Executive. In the background is the old order of Leeds buses, with 5284 NW and 5278 NW clearly visible. They were Leyland Titan PD3/5s, with Roe H38/32R bodywork, from a batch of thirty which were delivered to Leeds City Transport in March 1959. They had been taken into the fleet of West Yorkshire PTE in April 1974 but, by the time of the photograph, were about to be withdrawn. 5284 NW went on to operate in the fleet of Tyne and Wear PTE because of a vehicle shortage in the summer of 1976.

7 November 1976, The Gathering of the Atlanteans at Sovereign Street Depot

This line-up of Leyland Atlanteans with Roe bodywork, although looking very similar, has representatives from the Leeds City Transport fleet and vehicles new to West Yorkshire PTE. LUG 111P was the newest in the group, having been delivered to WYPTE in November 1975. UNW 412H was the oldest, having been new to Leeds City Transport in July 1970. JUG 514L had been delivered to Leeds in February 1973, while SUG 594M had been ordered by Leeds but delivered to WYPTE in May 1974. These vehicles were all to pass to Yorkshire Rider in October 1986.

October 1977, AEC Swift AUB 166J, Sheffield Pond Street Bus Station
AUB 166J was an AEC Swift with a Roe B48D body. It was one of a batch of twenty similar buses delivered new to Leeds City Transport in July 1971. It had been taken into the fleet of West Yorkshire PTE in April 1974 and continued in service for another ten years. It was seen in WYPTE livery loading passengers at Pond Street bus station, Sheffield.

September 1979, Leyland Atlantean JUG 521L Passes the Corn Exchange
JUG 521L was a Leyland Atlantean with a Roe H45/33D body. It was one of a batch of thirty-five similar buses which had been delivered to Leeds City Transport in the early part of 1973. They had all passed to the fleet of West Yorkshire PTE in April 1974. In 1979, JUG 521L was an early candidate for receiving the simplified WYPTE livery and would go on to outlive the PTE's bus operations by over two years when it passed to Yorkshire Rider in October 1986.

October 1980, Leyland Atlantean PDR1/1 CUB 331C, Leeds Central Bus Station
CUB 331C was a Leyland Atlantean PDR1/1 with a Weymann H41/29F body. It was the first of the Atlanteans delivered new to Leeds City Transport in July 1965 and marked the beginning of the end for the traditional rear-entrance buses in Leeds. In April 1974, it joined the West Yorkshire PTE fleet and continued in service for another eight years. It was purchased for preservation in July 1981 and can still be seen on the streets of West Yorkshire.

February 1984, Daimler Fleetlines, Torre Road Depot
JUM 222L, JUM 207L, JUM 214L and JUM 205L were Daimler Fleetlines with Roe H45/33D bodies. They were some of the batch of thirty delivered new to Leeds City Transport in the early part of 1972. All became part of the fleet of West Yorkshire PTE in April 1974. They were seen here in their last year of service with the PTE.

March 1984, Leyland Atlantean JUG 526L, Torre Road Depot
JUG 526L was a Leyland Atlantean PDR2/1 with a Roe H45/33D body. It had been delivered to new to Leeds City Transport in February 1973 and was one of a batch of thirty-five buses. It was taken into the fleet of West Yorkshire PTE in April 1974 and had another twelve years in service. Its final duties were as a play bus in the Halifax area.

April 1984, AUB 162J with KWY 239V, Leeds Central Bus Station
AUB 162J was another AEC Swift with a Roe B48D body from the batch of twenty similar buses delivered new to Leeds City Transport in July 1971. It had been taken into the fleet of West Yorkshire PTE in April 1974 and, after ten years' service with WYPTE, was a few months away from withdrawal when photographed. KWY 239V was a Leyland Atlantean AN68A/1R, with a Roe H43/32F body, which was delivered new to West Yorkshire PTE in June 1980. It would finally be withdrawn in September 2000.